LOVE THROUGH ALL SEASONS

*Growing Closer Together in
31 Days for a Lifetime*

S. L. BERGMANN

WESTBOW
P R E S S®
A DIVISION OF THOMAS NELSON
& ZONDERVAN

NIV: All Scripture quotations, unless otherwise indicated, are taken from the Holy Bible, New International Reader's Version®, NIrV® Copyright © 1995, 1996, 1998, 2014 by Biblica, Inc.™ Used by permission of Zondervan. All rights reserved worldwide. The "NIrV" and "New International Reader's Version" are trademarks registered in the United States Patent and Trademark Office by Biblica, Inc.

WestBow Press books may be ordered through booksellers or by contacting:

WestBow Press
A Division of Thomas Nelson & Zondervan
1663 Liberty Drive
Bloomington, IN 47403
www.westbowpress.com
1 (866) 928-1240

Because of the dynamic nature of the Internet, any web addresses or links contained in this book may have changed since publication and may no longer be valid. The views expressed in this work are solely those of the author and do not necessarily reflect the views of the publisher, and the publisher hereby disclaims any responsibility for them.

Any people depicted in stock imagery provided by Thinkstock are models, and such images are being used for illustrative purposes only. Certain stock imagery © Thinkstock.

ISBN: 978-1-9736-0738-0 (sc)
ISBN: 978-1-9736-0737-3 (e)

Library of Congress Control Number: 2017917366

Print information available on the last page.

WestBow Press rev. date: 12/06/2017

Contents

Strengthening Relationships

Destroying Relationships

Hope for the Broken Home

There is a time for everything,
and a season for every activity under the heavens.

ECCLESIASTES 3:1

To everything there is a season, in life and in relationships. We change, and every year is different than the last. My husband and I have had bright, sunny days and we've weathered the storms. One of the darkest clouds we've had remains, but we see the sun shining brightly in spite of it—he was diagnosed with Non-Hodgkins Lymphoma about fifteen years ago and is in remission. He considers having cancer a blessing. It has made him, he said, more appreciative of what he has and of life itself. It has made me realize although we go through all kinds of challenges life brings our way, we're in it together and I cherish each day I have with him—and I thank God for each day that I have him. We don't know what the future holds, but we know who holds the future.

If You are Not in a Relationship

Love Through All Seasons is for couples who are engaged and want to learn what it takes to have a successful relationship, or are already married and want to stay close through the changing seasons of their lives.

However, if you are single and want to find someone to share your life with, *Love Through All Seasons* will show you what entails a relationship in which love grows stronger over the years.

Choosing the Right Person

Love Through All Seasons focuses on placing God at the center of a relationship because He, as our Creator, is the author of Love. With Him as the foundation from which all of our decisions, dreams, hopes, direction and guidance are built upon ensures success.

Keeping this in mind, a successful relationship starts with the right kind of relationship. Through these pages you'll find the stark difference God makes in a relationship as opposed to how the world treats relationships, and how God serves as the glue to keeping a couple, and a family, together through life's challenges.

If you do not carefully choose the right person, chances are high the relationship will fail and you not only will be back to where you started from, you could be in a worse position than before that will leave you disillusioned. You may also develop distrust and fears to avoid being hurt again and harden your heart to protect yourself. It doesn't have to be that way. Here's how to avoid that.

The Mirage

Many want someone based on their looks or status, or both. The handsome model turns out to be an abuser. The trophy wife turns out to be shallow and a whiner. The gold digger finds out her husband is selfish and a cheater. The mansion turns out to be as cold as the marble pillars with rooms filled with loneliness and strife. Some even marry to gain citizenship or health insurance only to find themselves in a worse position than before. Famous couples are known for often having short marriages.

All either slowly, or quickly, die inside. With shattered expectations, some seek to figure out how to live in the midst of their existence, some divorce for a way out and others would rather not live.

What happened? Their faith and trust were on earthly things, not on God, whose principles are based on things that last.

Trusting God as Lord of your life, the first step is to look for someone whose heart is after God's. If we choose one whose heart is after God's we will be choosing someone who will bring sincere love into the relationship and help rule the home with the fruits of His spirit, which are: love, joy, peace, forbearance, kindness, goodness, faithfulness, gentleness and self-control (Galatians 5:22–23).

Forbearance means having patient self-control; restraint and tolerance. These are vital traits that help us during challenging times in a relationship and to rise above destructive tendencies that can destroy a relationship. Relationships often fail due to thoughtless impromptu actions. God is a spirit that lives inside us and transforms us to provide us with the will and strength to respond in love instead of hate.

As the spirit of God transforms a person, it also transforms a relationship. As we grow in God, His love is manifested in us and the fruits of His spirit grow stronger. When a couple places God in the center of their lives and have children, their children will taste the fruits and live in a home full of love, security, blessings, and peace.

Without God, there is just trust in the things that disillusion and decay. Don't fall for a mirage.

Also, when looking for someone to develop a relationship with, the Bible gives a strong command not to choose someone who doesn't believe in God, "Do not be yoked together with unbelievers. For what do righteousness and wickedness have in common? Or what fellowship can light have with darkness?" (2nd Corinthians 6:14).

For those who think this may not make a difference, examine the questions carefully.

One who is not of God can have a callous heart. Their priorities may be to manipulate and control, seek to harm physically and emotionally. They may have tendencies to be bitter and reside in anger, and be insensitive to the feelings and needs of others. Some hearts are so dark they revel in delivering cruelty to animals and people.

The one in God has a sincere, caring heart, strives to be obedient to Him and to do what is right, and take care to avoid causing pain. Their decisions will be based on following His commands which lead to a happier marriage and a stronger home.

Hence, *what do righteousness and wickedness have in common?* Many go into a relationship thinking they have enough in common and anything bad they can deal with—if it doesn't get worse, or will magically change for the better once they get married.

Consider the second question that addresses what kind of relationship one who lives in the light can have with one who lives in darkness. Both questions address a couple who are risking their quality of life, especially if they want to have children. An unstable home without a strong foundation can produce fractured lives.

Also, the questions apply to anyone, not just couples. Hooking up with the wrong kind of people can lead to problems you wish you didn't have.

When you consider someone to share your life with, choose carefully and thoughtfully. Examine their heart, actions and goals, and you'll see what kinds of seeds they will sow. In a relationship, you'll be sharing the kind of harvest that is produced. Will it be a garden of good fruit, or a ground of thorns?

The couple who sincerely love and follow God will find blessings in their relationship, and inside their home as well as outside. Obedience to God demonstrates love for Him, and genuine love to others provide a positive impact. Disobedience causes distrust and discord, inside the home as well as outside.

Love Through All Seasons demonstrates attitudes and traits that kill a relationship, as well as how real love removes fear and can grow richer, stronger, and last through all seasons.

Love Through All Seasons is more a resource for specific and common subjects than a devotional. It provides practical applications and thought-provoking questions to pull things into perspective and to apply them to encourage transformation away from what destroys relationships to grow closer to each other and God, for life. When the marriage and home life is strong, you'll discover it will be easier to have success outside the home.

Love Through All Seasons is ideal for anyone who wants to build a successful and enduring relationship. God is for relationships, because He is Love. He's given us the gift of life to have a relationship with Him, and with those he brings into our lives. His heart is poured out in the pages of the Bible of His plea for us to experience that rich love with Him and others to its fullest as He meant it to be. Only Satan stands in the way. As humans, our biggest challenge is to overcome the traps of destruction he sets to ensnare us in to keep us from each other and God. The Bible is the best source for solid instruction on how to avoid those traps and to build a relationship that lasts through the seasons of life. This book provides just a glimpse.

Strengthening Relationships

Day 1

The Definition of Love

Love is patient, love is kind.
It does not envy, it does not boast, it is not proud.
It does not dishonor others, it is not self-seeking,
it is not easily angered,
it keeps no record of wrongs.
Love does not delight in evil
but rejoices with the truth.
It always protects, always trusts,
always hopes, always perseveres.
Love never fails.

1 CORINTHIANS 13:4–8

Before proceeding with the rest of the book, it is ideal to take the time to thoroughly understand and appreciate what love means by reading the Bible's definition of love above. The rest of the book hinges on this definition. Memorize it. Realize how each truth would enrich your relationship. Imagine what a relationship would be like without each truth.

Day 2

Sincere Love

Love must be sincere. Hate what is evil; cling to what is good.
Be devoted to one another in love.
Honor one another above yourselves.

ROMANS 12:9–10

But the wisdom that comes from heaven is
first of all pure; then peace-loving,
considerate, submissive, full of mercy and
good fruit, impartial and sincere.

JAMES 3:17

Do nothing out of selfish ambition or vain conceit.
Rather in humility, value others above yourselves.

PHILIPPIANS 2:3

Be completely humble and gentle; be patient,
bearing with one another in love.

EPHESIANS 4:2

*Now that you have purified yourselves by obeying
the truth so that you have sincere love for each other,
love one another deeply, from the heart.*

1 PETER 1:22

*Greater love has no one than this: to lay
down one's life for one's friends.*

JOHN 15:13

Sincere love is demonstrated when you are willing to place your spouse's desire before your own. How can you lay your life down for your spouse? Discuss some ways you have done this before for each other, or ways you would appreciate your spouse laying down his or her life for you. For example, a wife tells her husband, "I know you want to watch the game, but we have been invited to my coworker's party. I really would like you to come with me." Think about what you'll lose by doing so, in comparison to what you would gain.

If you give up something for each other, you will gain a lot more than what you gave up.

Day 3

Love Does No Harm

*Let no debt remain outstanding, except the continuing
debt to love one another, for whoever loves others
has fulfilled the law. The commandments,
"You shall not commit adultery,"
"You shall not murder,"
"You shall not steal,"
"You shall not covet," and
whatever other command there may be,
are summed up in this one command:
"Love your neighbor as yourself."
Love does no harm to a neighbor.
Therefore love is the fulfillment of the law.*

ROMANS 13:8–10

"Love does no harm to a neighbor." That is the beauty of love—it does no harm.

The Ten Commandments are seen in many courthouses across the country. Many of our country's laws are based on the Bible, a reminder that God's laws were created to protect us. A violation of any commandment involves hurting someone. As a country stands

4

strong on biblical principles, so does a relationship. God's goal was with Moses, as it is with us today, to save us from destroying ourselves and each other. In a relationship and marriage, the couple should protect each other.

Read the Ten Commandments in Exodus 20 or Deuteronomy 5 thoughtfully, and reflect on what would happen to your marriage, your life, and your relationship with God if you did the opposite of each commandment.

> *In fact, this is love for God: to keep his commands.*
> *And his commands are not burdensome.*
>
> 1 JOHN 5:3

> *For my yoke is easy, and my burden is light.*
>
> MATTHEW 11:30

Satan is known as the deceiver and destroyer, and he is bent on destroying our lives spiritually, mentally, emotionally, and physically. He lures people with illusions that will ultimately ensnare and destroy them, and their relationships inside the home as well as outside. Evil will promise you one thing but deliver another. You were promised easy and safe money but landed in jail for fraud. You needed a quick mental escape but became addicted to drugs. You wanted revenge but sit on death row for murder.

The Bible was written thousands of years ago and still holds timeless truths to avoid deadly snares. God's promises still stand true. He never changes, his light is bright as the sword of truth, and His wisdom protects those who cling to His Word. He listens to those who turn to Him. His gifts bless those who follow Him. When we stay on His path, our road will be well lit and on solid ground.

When we stray, we see shadows. The farther we stray, the more we grow in darkness.

Those who turn to destructive things lose their sleep with worry, lose themselves and their relationships, and might even lose their lives. They carry baggage so heavy they are weighed down by their burdens. Sometimes it is not easy to follow what God wants, but it leads to a much easier life. Your relationship will have much fewer problems. Each day presents enough challenges on its own. His ways do not cause harm. His way gives life, not death. His burden is light. Hell makes you pay.

Day 4

Perfect Love

*Above all, love each other deeply, because
love covers over a multitude of sins.*

1 PETER 4:8

*Dear friends, since God so loved us, we also ought to love one another.
No one has ever seen God; but if we love one another,
God lives in us and his love is made complete in us.*

1 JOHN 4:11–12

*And so we know and rely on the love God has for us. God is love.
Whoever lives in love lives in God, and God in them.*

1 JOHN 4:16

Therefore, as God's chosen people, holy and dearly loved,
clothe yourselves with compassion, kindness, humility,
gentleness and patience. Bear with each other and forgive one
another if any of you has a grievance against someone.
Forgive as the Lord forgave you. And over all these virtues put
on love, which binds them all together in perfect unity.

COLLOSSIANS 3:12-14

There is no fear in love. But perfect love drives out
fear, because fear has to do with punishment.
The one who fears is not made perfect in love.

1 JOHN 4:18

Discuss with each other why some people are afraid of love and how perfect love removes fear.

In the definition of love as described in Corinthians, and at the beginning of the day 1 chapter in this book, you can see why there is no fear in love and how perfect love casts out fear. We all have fear and insecurities at some level within us, because we all sin and live in a world full of sin. Those who mistreat others torment them without cause verbally, emotionally, and physically. Fear sends an alarm throughout our bodies. When we fear, we're afraid of being harmed. But when we grow in God, we become more like Him; His love grows within us and we overcome our fears. When we share that love with others, we dissolve their fears too. Satan torments. God's love does not.

Since God is love, when you love others, they see a reflection of Him in you. They know they can trust in Him as opposed to the Prince of Darkness who deceives everyone with lies and fills them with hate. The ones who do not love live in darkness, and if they live in a world full of darkness, they remain lost and search for things to fill the void inside. You can be that light and share real love that many in this world are not accustomed to. In a relationship, real love—caring, sincere, and placing others before ourselves—is transforming and elevating, making each year stronger than the last and withstanding the tests of time. God softens the heart. Satan hardens it.

God's commandments are based on love. If everyone did so, what a different world we would have. Hate would cease. Fear would be gone. Demonstrating love would be like bringing heaven to earth and the home.

Day 5

Preventing Escalation

Make sure that nobody pays back wrong for
wrong, but always strive to do what is good for
each other and for everyone else.

1 THESSALONIANS 5:15

Evil will never leave the house of one who pays back evil for good.

PROVERBS 17:13

For the entire law is fulfilled in keeping this one command:
"Love your neighbor as yourself."
If you bite and devour each other, watch out or
you will be destroyed by each other.

GALATIANS 5:14–15

When our spouses hurt our feelings, it can be easy to want to retaliate and to make them hurt. But if we do that, we ultimately hurt ourselves more. Do whatever is possible to maintain peace in your relationship. God's love for us by demonstrating patience and forgiveness is a model to follow on how we treat each other. Instead of using sarcasm or a sharp retort, Proverbs 15:1 notes, "A gentle answer turns away wrath, but a harsh word stirs up anger."

We often say things we regret. Statements that pierce another's heart. The wrong words can break a marriage, destroy a friendship, and tear families apart. Lies and slander can ruin lives. Vulnerable teens and adults alike have committed suicide over hurtful words said about them. Sometimes it is just *how* it is said that makes the difference. Don't add gasoline to the fire. Give a soft answer instead of grievous words. Doing so can calm the issue and even immediately flip the situation around. Respond with kindness and thoughtfulness. We show love to others by how we respond to them. A thoughtless retort given in a second can result in a lifetime of regret. Hate is strong, but love improves the outcome and becomes stronger.

Satan tears apart a marriage, a family. Christ keeps a marriage together.

Satan tells us to hurt someone else. Christ says, "Love one another."

Satan tells us to take revenge. Christ said, "Love your enemies, be good to those that hurt you."

Satan spurs us to do evil deeds. Christ spurs us to do good.

Satan enslaves us. Christ frees us.

Satan destroys our lives. Christ saves.

As part of the Parables in Matthew 5:9 Jesus had said, "Blessed are the peacemakers." Your home, your marriage will flourish with the strength of peace. Use the same energy you would to respond in anger by responding in love instead. This pivotal action changes the course of your relationship to make it weaker or stronger.

Day 6

Love as Christ Loved Us

*Husbands, love your wives, just as Christ loved
the church and gave himself up for her.*

EPHESIANS 5:25

*Be kind and compassionate to one another, forgiving
each other, just as in Christ God forgave you.*

EPHESIANS 4:32

*Accept one another, then, just as Christ accepted
you, in order to bring praise to God.*

ROMANS 15:7

*A new command I give you: Love one another.
As I have loved you, so you must love one another.*

JOHN 13:34

My command is this: Love each other as I have loved you.

JOHN 15:12

Jesus tells us twice to love each other as He loved us, emphasizing the importance of how we should love each other. Your spouse may do things that annoy you and make mistakes. The Bible doesn't say to hold a grudge or to be bitter—it says to be kind, tenderhearted and forgiving. Love does not keep a record of wrongs. When we ask God for forgiveness, not only does He forgive us, the Bible says He remembers our sins no more. The home should be a sanctuary, not a place of condemnation. Christ said He came to save the world, not to condemn it (John 3:17, & 12:47).

Think about ways Jesus has demonstrated His love to us, and how you can apply this to your relationship.

One significant example of how Jesus's demonstration of love can help change someone's perspective of you and increase trust is revealed in John 18:10. When the soldiers came to arrest Jesus that would eventually lead him to his torture and death sentence, Simon Peter cut off one of the servant's ear to try to prevent the arrest of Jesus. Jesus scolded him. With kindness, he healed the man's ear. No anger, no bitterness, no revenge. Just love. It didn't stop his arrest or death on the cross, but imagine how that one act of kindness may have changed the servant's perspective—and even his life. Jesus was consistent throughout his life in showing love.

Day 7

Seeing Good Days

If it is possible, as far as it depends on you, live at peace with everyone.

ROMANS 12:18

Read each sentence thoughtfully and carefully:

Finally, all of you, be like-minded, be sympathetic,
love one another, be compassionate and humble.
Do not repay evil with evil or insult with insult.
On the contrary, repay evil with blessing,
because to this you were called so that you may inherit a blessing.
For,
"Whoever would love life and see good days
must keep their tongue from evil
and their lips from deceitful speech.
They must turn from evil and do good
they must seek peace and pursue it.
For the eyes of the Lord are on the righteous
and his ears are attentive to their prayer,
but the face of the Lord is against those who do evil."

1 PETER 3:8–12

1. What does the verse say you will inherit if you do as it instructs? Compare the possible aftermaths of repaying evil for evil, or heaping insults on each other, to the promise of receiving a blessing.
2. What does it mean to seek peace and pursue it? How do you pursue peace?

One way to chase after peace is to hold your tongue from retorting, however hard it may be. As Christians—Christ followers—we are to follow His example and live as He did. He lived in a world that constantly scorned Him. Yet He always responded with love. He encouraged others to love, even their enemies, and to be peacemakers.

Parents are often called to be the referee of their children's fights, and many respond by saying, "I don't care who started it, I care more about you two making up for it." Teachers and coaches intervene to break up a fight. But if a couple are fighting with no one to intervene, being the first to be a peacemaker is more than a condition of the heart. It is taking on the responsibility of choosing to do what God wants and placing love first, instead of giving into an impulsive negative response that adds fuel to the fire.

Such responses may be judging others instead of taking the time to understand and build a bridge to them. Others put up walls. Some send an email that causes discord. One click of the mouse is all it takes instead of delivering a fist—the result is the same. Being a peacemaker is a great responsibility, and opportunity, to keep love alive.

Day 8

Making the Goal Together

*Then make my joy complete by being like-minded, having
the same love, being one in spirit and of one mind.*

PHILIPPIANS 2:2

*So that there should be no division in the body, but that
its parts should have equal concern for each other.*

1 CORINTHIANS 12:25

*Where there is strife, there is pride, but wisdom
is found in those who take advice.*

PROVERBS 13:10

Plans fail for lack of counsel, but with many advisers they succeed.

PROVERB 15:22

Each day has its challenges with decisions to make and problems
to solve. The special part of being a married is you don't have to
deal with the big issues alone. When a decision needs to be made,

a strong marriage entails considering each other's concerns and working together to find a solution.

Many of us like to think we don't need to consult with anyone. That's pride, and a dangerous perception. Whether it is trying to decide what course to take when a decision needs to be made—how to settle a dispute, making plans for building a house—research, consulting with others, and planning with the new knowledge will produce a more successful outcome. Those who seek to gain wisdom and understanding are far ahead and better prepared than those who prefer to close their minds to anything beyond that which they can see or relate to.

It also is a matter of respect to each other to consult with each other. The bond is deepened and trust is gained. To do otherwise shows lack of consideration.

Because there is real power in prayer, ask God to help you both to be like-minded, to be of one spirit and to share the same purpose to meet the goal. If we only relied upon our limited understanding and thoughts we would be setting ourselves up for failure. If there is an impasse, seek counsel from those you trust. Another may bring to light what you might not have considered.

When you work as a team, imagine what you both can accomplish together. It is also better make the goal together than to be on opposite teams.

Day 9

A Man and Woman Complete Each Other

*Nevertheless, in the Lord, however,
woman is not independent of man,
nor is man independent of woman.
For as woman came from man,
so also man is born of woman.
But everything comes from God.*

1 CORINTHIANS 11:11–12

Marriage is a special opportunity to help balance each other, to deal with things inside the home, as well as outside. God made man and woman each with their own strength that are unique as a male and female. Men have qualities women don't, and vice versa, but the two together provide a whole solution. This applies to raising your children, how you look at problems and solve them, how you help pull things into perspective.

We change as the seasons change, and each year produces its own weather. Sunny days, stormy days, brutal hot days, extreme cold days. Because you are married you take on the storms together, and shelter each other. You tackle the world's problems together, everything is together and you work to help complete the missing pieces we all have—from our childhood, to our everyday life, and how we change through life. The goal is to weather the seasons together under the umbrella of God.

Day 10

The Perfect Companion

Read Genesis 2:18–24, the story of Adam and Eve.

Adam was given the responsibility of naming all the animals, birds and every living creature. Adam must have noticed they all were male and female and had a very special relationship. They played with each other, they had sex and created more of their kind. He watched them take care of their young ones, and how they grew up as a family. Adam didn't have a mate to enjoy life with.

God noticed it was not good for Adam to be alone and created a suitable helper for him and one who would help bring balance to his life. By taking a rib from Adam he created a woman with it and brought her to him. She was, literally, a part of him. By joining him to share life together, they formed a special, unique relationship that God had infused in all of His living creatures.

That is why a man leaves his father and mother and
is united to his wife, and they become one flesh.
GENESIS 2:24, MATTHEW 19:5, EPHESIANS 5:31

Sometimes in a marriage a spouse may feel alone, even though they live together. Do you feel alone in your relationship? Discuss this with each other in a loving, caring manner, and together come up with solutions.

The tale of two couples

At the end of the same day, two different outcomes for two couples.

It was a perfect weather on a Saturday. Not too hot or cool. The first husband gave up his time to play golf and instead play catch with his son. He asked his wife what kind of help she wanted him to do around the house, and he was happy to oblige. It didn't matter how hard the task, or menial, it was helping her. He then took her out to dinner. When they returned from dinner, their son had questions on his homework and he enjoyed helping him to learn how to solve his problems. The family went to bed content and slept peacefully. Tomorrow would bear the fruits of the seeds he planted today.

The second husband denied his son's request to play catch so he could golf instead, he couldn't pass up the perfect weather. He ignored and criticized his wife when she asked him if he could help with some things that needed to be done around the house. This escalated into a fight. He stormed out of the house and didn't come home for dinner. The mother helped her son with his homework. He came home very late and surly, and said the next day he would be taking a motorcycle ride by himself. The mother and son felt like they walked on eggshells at home. They all went to bed unhappy. Tomorrow would bear the fruits of the seeds he planted today. Note this is a soft example, some families have it much worse.

The perfect companion demonstrates real love, adheres to God's commands to serve and love the other to the fullest. By fulfilling each other's needs, they grow content and closer. They become one.

Day 11

Joy and Sorrow

*Isaac brought her into the tent of his mother
Sarah, and he married Rebekah.
So she became his wife, and he loved her; and Isaac
was comforted after his mother's death.*

GENESIS 24:67

Marriage is a special relationship through joy and sorrow. God is
into relationships, and a special part of having a relationship is so
we could provide comfort to each other, and so that we would not
have to deal with life's pains alone. Some don't know how to comfort
others and may find it awkward. Share with your spouse how you
like to be comforted. Sometimes it is just support in silence. Take
the time to comfort each other when needed.

We all experience the death of a family member or friend. Life also
brings us experiences which cause us to mourn—the loss of a job, or
we didn't get the promotion. A natural disaster destroyed our home
and everything inside we cherished. We just discovered we have
cancer, or one close to us.

Our spouse serves a special role to step in closer to us to offer comfort, support and to help lift us up so we can carry on. This helps to give us strength to overcome the grief. We are also given that special opportunity to help comfort and strengthen our spouse. Part of God's design in creating us is He made us to love each other and to comfort each other during life's most painful times.

What makes a marriage special is the commitment to stay with each other until death. Marriage is also designed for a family. Just as a wife and husband are there for each other, they are also there for their children to share in victories as well as to dry an eye, to comfort them when they are scared or dealing with painful issues. Our deep love for our spouse and children are modeled after God's love for us—to bless, comfort, protect, strengthen, encourage, provide, and to rejoice through the seasons of our lives.

Day 12

Romance and Intimacy

Romance is important in a relationship and enhances it

Enjoy life with your wife, whom you love.

ECCLESIASTES 9:9

The first part of this verse says it all. Enjoy life with your spouse. Having intimacy and passion are essential to enriching a relationship. For many couples it can grow dim over time. Discuss ways you would like to have intimacy and romance in your relationship. It doesn't have to cost much, and can be as simple as eating dinner by candlelight and playing soft music. God created us to be intimate with each other. Watch how male and female ducks stay close to each other, how the male watches over the female. How she is his companion. How they balance each other to raise their family and to survive through life. Revel in that special power of closeness and find ways to keep passion strong through time.

— It is easy to get caught up in your children's activities. Being involved in their lives is crucial, but don't become so involved you neglect your spouse while you are raising your children and lose connection with each other.

— Date and touch base often to keep on top of the changes you both go through in life. Let their grandparents spend quality time with them so you can have quality time together, or hire a baby sitter on a regular basis.

— Remain as a team. Your children will come and go, and leave the nest one day. Your spouse will still be there, and better to have your best friend there, than someone you don't know.

— Through life, we change as the seasons change. If you keep up with each other and adapt as a couple, your life and love together can grow richer, deeper, and stronger through these changes.

You can never say "I Love You" too many times.

Day 13

Treating Your Spouse

Husbands, love your wives and do not be harsh with them.

COLOSSIANS 3:19

*The King will reply, 'Truly I tell you, whatever
you did for one of the least of these
brothers and sisters of mine, you did for me.'*

MATTHEW 25:40

*He will reply, 'Truly I tell you, whatever you did not do
for one of the least of these, you did not do for me.'*

MATTHEW 25:45

When a person's heart hurts, God's heart hurts because He loves and cares about each of us. When we cause someone to grieve, we grieve God. That is why there are many verses throughout the Bible that talks of taking care of how we treat each other, because according to Jesus, it is how we treat Him. Many couples treat their friends and strangers better than their spouse

When we marry, we make a choice to love and serve each other for life, a very special commitment that is recognized by God and witnessed by His heavenly hosts, as well as those on earth, and in Satan's realm. God meant for marriage to be a joyful union and to stay united through the tests of time. Satan seeks to destroy what God ordains, and plants thoughts of bitterness and seeds of strife to decay the relationship and end the union. The two verses above remind us to stay committed and focused on love. When we love our spouse, we are loving God, who provides what is sincere and lasting.

Day 14

What Women and Men Want

Each one of you must also love his wife as he loves himself, and the wife must respect her husband.

EPHESIANS 5:33

Long before relationship experts and talk show hosts proclaimed that women have a strong need to know they are loved, and that reverence—deep respect—is important to a man, the Bible confirmed these facts thousands of years ago.

Examine these truths and see the value of applying them to your relationship. How do these two approaches for the husband and wife enrich the relationship? What do you envision if the opposite were to happen? For example, not being submissive can range from not listening to outright rebellion.

What does it mean if a man loves his wife, he loves himself?

Day 15

Hindered Prayers

As a wife is to show respect to her husband, the husband likewise is to show her respect.

Husbands, in the same way be considerate as you live with your wives, and treat them with respect as the weaker partner and as heirs with you of the gracious gift of life, so that nothing will hinder your prayers.

1 PETER 3:7

Did you catch that? *"... so that nothing will hinder your prayers."*

The wife is considered the weaker vessel as her physical strength is not made like a man's, and he shouldn't take advantage of her, but consider her as an equal in God's eyes as both of you are important to Him. Your strength is to help serve and protect her. Love her, and work with her in life to grow closer to God, to each other, and trusting God with everyday situations. You both are heirs <u>together</u> of the gracious gift of life!

For the wife and husband, if you are wondering why God isn't 'listening' to you in prayer...are you listening to God? Examine the areas of your key responsibilities—first yourself to Him, then your relationship with your spouse, children, job, etc. It all starts with you, and your responsibilities reflect you. If you take care of what God has entrusted you with, you will see blessings abound in your life, and the fruits of the spirit grow in your home.

Day 16

Winning Your Spouse Over

Wives, in the same way submit yourselves to your own husbands
so that, if any of them do not believe the word, they may be
won over without words by the behavior of their wives.

1 PETER 3:1

Do you know of someone who has gotten to know the Lord through their spouse? It does work. Unfortunately, many have called themselves Christians but have made God look bad through their fallen behavior and turned them off to God. Your wisdom and devotion will increase their confidence in you. The Bible says the spouse can have the influence to show the real Christ and the greatness of His love. If your spouse is an unbeliever, hold steadfast in prayer, be patient, let your speech and attitude reflect the Savior you adore, introduce biblical wisdom as solutions into situations and in due time your spouse will see God revealed as you manifest His glory. Love your spouse with the sincere love that God gives us, and not as the world gives—your spouse will experience the difference.

Day 17

The Successful Wife

A wife of noble character is her husband's crown, but
a disgraceful wife is like decay in his bones.

PROVERBS 12:4

Houses and wealth are inherited from parents,
but a prudent wife is from the Lord.

PROVERBS 19:14

A sum of different dictionary definitions define prudent as one who shows care and thought for the future, one who carefully provides for the future, is marked by wisdom, and shrewd in the management of practical affairs. House and wealth, although inherited, can be lost through bad management. This verse points out a good hearted, sincere spouse from God cares deeply about preserving what God has entrusted them with, and plans ahead to ensure the home and its inhabitants are taken care of.

One who does not believe in God can do just as well, the difference is the trust, wisdom and strength comes from God in the preservation that overcomes what Satan seeks to destroy. Money and material things can disappear, and the faith that is stored in it disappears as well. Faith and trust in God who hears those who listen to him will have solid protection.

Choosing a spouse who trusts in God is choosing a spouse who will give to a relationship, not take away, because their heart is after God's, which is kind, loving and sincere, and seeks to preserve.

He who finds a wife finds what is good and receives favor from the Lord.

PROVERBS 18:22

The wise woman builds her house, but with her own hands the foolish one tears hers down.

PROVERBS 14:1

Discuss this together to learn from each other's perspective:

1. How a wise woman can build her home.

2. How a foolish one can tear hers down.

Proverbs 31:10–31 describes the character of the successful wife.

In summary, her husband has full confidence in her, she brings him good and not harm. She plans ahead, is enterprising and that her trading is profitable. She is frugal and when she earns money—she doesn't waste it, she invests it. She is sincere in her love, willing to work hard and long hours. She is compassionate and cares about others, prepares for the future, and helps her husband to be successful. She makes sure her family and servants are taken care of and don't lack in any need, and she isn't afraid to do what it takes to make sure their needs are met. She is wise, kind, aware of what needs to be done, works to make others look good, doesn't waste her time, is blessed by her family, and people praise her for her hard and unselfish efforts.

These qualities are also qualities that make people successful in the workplace.

Day 18

Gaining Approval

If your brother or sister is distressed because of what you eat,
you are no longer acting in love.
Do not by your eating destroy someone for whom Christ died.
Therefore do not let what you know is good be spoken of as evil.
For the kingdom of God is not a matter of eating and drinking,
but of righteousness, peace and joy in the Holy Spirit,
because anyone who serves Christ in this way
is pleasing to God and receives human approval.

ROMANS 14:15–18

Yesterday you read about the attributes that make a successful wife. In Proverbs 31 verses 28 and 29 address how her husband and family perceive her: Her children arise and call her blessed; her husband also, and he praises her: "Many women do noble things, but you surpass them all."

Self-esteem is important, but it is more important to strive for God's approval, and if you do all that He commands you, you will gain your family's approval. Encourage each other. When you do what is praiseworthy—you, and your spouse, will reap from the goodness you have sown together.

Many believe that to gain approval and marital success the answer lies in achieving a certain status and having expensive things, without realizing these are things that may not last. They also may find in pursuing such things may not help them reach their ideal goal.

Some push their husbands to have a higher position in the company so they can keep up with the Joneses, but fail to realize this can result in more hours he is away from her and their children and have to deal with the stress he unloads at home. They don't consider the Joneses also may be on their way to bankruptcy.

Some want to buy more expensive items and clothes, and have what they deem a prestigious status in society, only to find out whom they thought were their friends will gossip and stab them in the back.

Those who are after God's heart follow Him to love and do no harm, strive to elevate and build each other up, and place faith in Him because what He holds is what lasts. Those who are of the world couldn't care less and stumble.

Top hero movies of today present heroes and heroines who are not afraid to fight evil and stand up for what is right, and fight injustice. The heroes represent those who value what many of us do, can relate to and want, but cannot. Because of peer pressure with the wrong kind of friends, fighting temptation or just feeling unable to triumph over what pushes us to do wrong seems too hard to fight against. For many, the antagonists represent the antagonists in our lives, and we cheer to see one who can fight and overcome the oppressor.

A mark of one whose heart is after God strengthens themselves in His Word to fight injustice and make decisions that lead to a better outcome. This is an everyday battle in this world for those who want truth to win and God's laws to prevail.

Such bravery is not impossible. For one who grows in God sees the difference and feels the strength to overcome. Some have experienced it so far as Jonathan did in the book of Samuel. The enemy had a camp on the other side of the garrison. Because Jonathan had built a relationship with God, he told his armor bearer if the enemy were to respond in one way, they would back off, but if they were to respond in another way, they would proceed to attack. Just he and his armor bearer, who vowed to help no matter the cost.

When they received the clue that they could attack, they forged ahead and just the two, with God's help, won the battle against the many men. The same happened to David who fought Goliath. Such can happen to us as we fight our own battles that threaten to destroy what we cherish when we include our Creator and fight for what is good.

It is easy to yearn for the approval of others, but their approval can be fleeting. We may be popular one day, forgotten the next. But as we seek to win the approval of God by loving Him and each other, we make a real difference and build good memories that can last a lifetime.

Gaining approval inside the home is important, but also outside of the home as well. How you consider others outside the home impacts relationships with them and your relationship with God. The consequences, negative or positive, can be brought into the home.

We who are strong ought to bear with the failings
of the weak and not to please ourselves.
Each of us should please his neighbors for his good, to build them up.
ROMANS 15:1–2

37

Even as I try to please everyone in every way.
For I am not seeking my own good
but the good of many, so that they may be saved.

1 CORINTHIANS 10:33

Compliment your spouse every day. When your spouse does something that makes the day easier, your lives better, praise your spouse for that. Build each other up, don't tear each other down. If you spend each day loving each other, insecurity will change to security.

Day 19

Helping Others Together

She opens her arms to the poor and extends her hands to the needy.

PROVERBS 31:20

Jesus said we are to feed the poor and care for the widows and orphans (help those who cannot help themselves). As a couple, what can you do to help others? Talk to your pastor and offer your time and services to help someone who could use your help. You could do things such as paint a fence, tutor a struggling student, house repairs for an elderly senior—life's list of needs is countless.

An act of kindness does not go unnoticed by those whose lives it impacts and can be remembered forever.

Pray and discuss what situations you feel you can best assist. Help is needed everywhere. Consider this as a venture you share together, you will find joy as you do so. Joy for the person whom you help, joy inside yourself for pleasing God, and joy with your spouse as you do something worthwhile together. As you grow together through life you can look back and feel good about those in whose lives you have made a difference as the power of a couple, and reflect on the power of love.

Day 20

Going the Extra Mile

And whatever you do, whether in word or deed, do it all in the name of the Lord Jesus, giving thanks to God the Father through him.

COLOSSIANS 3:17

This verse points out whatever you do, do it for God and with thankfulness. If your spouse wants you to do an extra chore when you would rather watch television, remember it is the Lord you serve, and when you serve Him, you are also serving your spouse with love, and your relationship with both are strengthened.

Everything we have, every opportunity given to us, is by His hand. How hard are we willing to work for the God who made us and provides for us? The presentation is okay, but would a little more time added to it make the difference between a nod and an applause? The floor is swept, but would mopping it make it shine? The project boring, but someone needs it done, and by tomorrow. It is more than our employer we are serving, it is God.

When we realize that the outcome of a project is really a reflection of us and our dedication, and whom we are serving, then it will matter. Our actions will turn to a labor of love. Not only will God approve—whomever we are serving such as our spouse or employer—would take notice and appreciate, too. As we take care of the smallest things well, God will entrust us with greater responsibilities, just as our employer will. Whomever we serve, if we serve as if we are serving God, how can we lose?

Marriage is not giving 50%–50%, it is giving 100%–100%. You give it your all.

Day 21

Meekness and Gentleness

Two strengths that make the relationship stronger.

Meekness is self-control. It is not to be wimpy or timid. It is an essential strength and the Bible says the meek will inherit the earth. Those who gain self-control preserve peace, as well as foster stability and strength. A fool is one who cannot control himself and leaves a trail of destruction. Meekness in a marriage is having the strength to prevent an argument from cycling and spiraling downward. It is responding in love instead of lashing back. It is fighting destructive temptations and having the temperance to be even-keeled and steady. When you grow in God you will find the power to do these things. When you grow in Him and develop the fruits of His spirit, love and harmony will guide your actions and prevail in your home.

Gentleness may not be considered a masculine trait but the strength and power of being gentle for both husband and wife is stronger than iron. A gentle response adds water to the fire instead of gasoline, a gentle touch can calm. How does a hurting animal respond and trust? By a gentle person. Handling your spouse with gentleness shows consideration, respect and compassion, and is the essence of caring.

DESTROYING RELATIONSHIPS

Day 22

Dissension

Dissension with each other is dissention with God.

Therefore, if you are offering your gift
at the altar and there remember
that your brother or sister has something against you,
leave your gift there in front of the altar. First go and be
reconciled to them; then come and offer your gift.
Matthew 5:23–24

Reconciliation is huge to God. He wants us to be reconciled to the one we have offended, and even to one who has offended us. He would rather have us patch things up with our spouse, THEN go to Him.

Reconciliation begins with an apology to one we have wronged with a sincere attempt to make things right; just as we apologize to God and repent to show our sincerity. Forgiveness is the next step to move the relationship forward. As God forgives us, we are to forgive. To be forgiven is great, to forgive is even greater.

Each situation we face is a trial at hand. One of the greatest challenges one can have is to hold their tongue in a dispute. When in such a trying situation, first ask yourself, "Will this problem bring me closer to God, or away from Him?" How we respond will determine that course.

You may find if you make decisions that take you away from Him, they may also cause division with your spouse.

Our first inclination may be to take revenge but the Bible warns us against this and advises: Do not take revenge, my dear friends, but leave room for God's wrath, for it is written: "It is mine to avenge; I will repay," says the Lord (Romans 12:19).

Remember, His ways are higher than our ways. Before you wait and expect to watch the one who wronged you really get it from God, realize God may be working in their life in ways you won't expect. There may have been times you have experienced God's mercy when you didn't deserve it, and His correction when you did. He shows mercy to those who show others mercy. He is interested in their redemption more than He is interested in their destruction. His justice and timetable is fair.

Love is liberating. Hate and revenge calls for a chain of actions that keeps everyone involved hostage in bitterness and anger that lead to destruction.

If a house be divided against itself, that house cannot stand.

MARK 3:25

Whoever would foster love covers over an offense, but whoever repeats the matter separates close friends.

PROVERBS 17:9

For if you forgive other people when they sin against you, your heavenly Father will also forgive you. But if you do not forgive others their sins, your Father will not forgive your sins.

MATTHEW 6:14–15

Hatred stirs up conflict, but love covers over all wrongs.

PROVERBS 10:12

Be the first to love and move the relationship forward.

Day 23

It IS What You Say

Although it is true actions speak louder than words, words trigger emotion and action.

Many verses talk about how people use words as weapons and controlling what we say. Spouses are supposed to be for each other, not against each other. God instructs us to build each other up, not tear each other down. God is the author of love, and when you place Him first you will be placing each other first—let love dominate your relationship.

If you have a habit of unloading your stress on your spouse and being negative, critical, and abusive to help you 'feel better'—you won't—and it will build up onto the next day and each day will grow darker for both of you. What starts at the home is carried out to other areas.

Today start with prayer asking God to help you heal your bitterness and to help you seek ways to stop the stream of hurt. Ask your spouse to forgive you. Whenever your spouse asks you for forgiveness, forgive as Christ forgives you when you ask for forgiveness, and repent. Don't return the negative attitude. Promote peace and respond with love.

The tongue has the power of life and death,
and those who love it will eat its fruit.

PROVERBS 18:21

Likewise the tongue is a small part of the
body, but it makes great boasts.
Consider what a great forest is set on fire by a small spark.

JAMES 3:5

Gracious words are a honeycomb, sweet to
the soul and healing to the bones.

PROVERBS 16:24

The tongue also is a fire, a world of evil among the parts of the body.
It corrupts the whole body, sets the whole course of
one's life on fire and is itself set on fire by hell.

JAMES 3:6

What goes into someone's mouth does not defile them, but
what comes out of their mouth, that is what defiles them.

MATTHEW 15:11

The words of a gossip are like choice morsels;
they go down to the inmost parts.

PROVERBS 26:22

Do not slander one another.
Anyone who speaks against a brother or sister or judges them
speaks against the law and judges it. When you judge the
law, you are not keeping it, but sitting in judgment on it.

JAMES 4:11

A marriage can deteriorate over time when spouses cannot control their tongue and choose to unleash language that disrespects, condescends and wounds the soul. Words spoken in anger cannot be taken back, no matter how much we wish they could be. The effect of one hurtful statement can linger for years—even a lifetime.

The Bible is clear on how we treat others and the consequences:

But I tell you that anyone who is angry with his
brother or sister will be subject to judgment.
Again, anyone who says to his brother or sister,
'Raca,' is answerable to the court. But anyone who says,
'You fool!' will be in danger of the fire of hell.

MATTHEW 5:22

Raca is a derogatory expression said with contempt and implies a person is stupid, worthless and inferior. An example is when a spouse expresses unrighteous anger and unleashes condescending, hateful remarks without remorse to the other. God is very clear on where he stands with such attitudes.

Words can hurt and destroy. We have experienced the harmful power the tongue can have. It can bring life, or it can destroy a life. The tongue is not the largest member of our body, but it is one that can do the most damage. We can change lives by our actions, we can also change lives by what we say.

Day 24

Quarreling

*Better to live on a corner of the roof than share
a house with a quarrelsome wife.*

PROVERBS 21:9 AND PROVERBS 25:24

*As charcoal to embers and as wood to fire, so is
a quarrelsome person for kindling strife.*

PROVERBS 26:21

*A quarrelsome wife is like a constant dripping
of a leaky roof in a rainstorm.*

PROVERBS 27:15

A complainer does not sit well with God, nor others. To complain about a situation and seek justice, or a solution, is natural and proactive. But constant complaining to others saps their energy, and as a Christian this is denouncing God because it is saying God is ineffective and not helpful. Complaining demonstrates lack of love to others and God. Satan depreciates us. God elevates us.

It is to one's honor to avoid strife, but every fool is quick to quarrel.

PROVERBS 20:3

⌐

Without wood a fire goes out; without gossip a quarrel dies down.

PROVERBS 26:20

⌐

Starting a quarrel is like breaching a dam; so drop the matter before a dispute breaks out.

PROVERBS 17:14

Stress often triggers quarrels. We live in a world that easily stresses us out. The headlines screaming catastrophes, the annoying neighbor, the stock market, the team that screwed up, the ticking deadline, the political games, and the list goes on. Tune out the world and tune into what God says.

Wherever you are—whether you're waiting in line or in a doctor's office—use that time to pray about your concerns and place them in His lap. Count your blessings and what you are thankful for. Also, think of things that relax you. Read Philippians 4:8 (also shown at the end of Day 26), this verse is a good one to memorize and go line by line when you are in the slow moving, mile-long traffic. The difference in how you feel may show by the time you get to work or home.

It takes two to quarrel, and both spouses are equally responsible to diffuse it. The one who responds with love holds the greater weight to make the relationship last. Love preserves. Bitterness decays.

Day 25

Anger

"In your anger do not sin": Do not let the sun go down while you are still angry, and do not give the devil a foothold.

EPHESIANS 4:26–27

It is natural to feel angry at times, we all do. But don't carry your anger over into the next day. A foothold is a secure place for the feet, such as for a rock climber before he can make the next ascent. Don't let the devil cause you to lose ground. Clinging to anger and revenge will rot your mind and body. Not only does it place a distance between you and your spouse, it also puts a distance between you and God. Satan says, "Hold on and get back." God says, "Let go, and let me take care of it." Initiate peace, right a wrong. Start the next day with a fresh slate, and a clean heart. Each day you have is a gift. It is too valuable to waste it on what can cripple your future. Focus on rebuilding instead of destroying.

Do not be quickly provoked in your spirit, for anger resides in the lap of fools.

ECCLESIASTES 7:9

Mockers stir up a city, but wise men turn away anger.

PROVERBS 29:8

An angry person stirs up conflict, and a hot-tempered person commits many sins.

PROVERBS 29:22

*My dear brothers and sisters, take note of this:
Everyone should be quick to listen, slow to speak and
slow to become angry, because human anger does not
produce the righteous life that God desires.*

JAMES 1:19–20

*A hot-tempered man stirs up conflict, but the
one who is patient calms a quarrel.*

PROVERBS 15:18

*The wise fear the Lord and shun evil, but a fool is hotheaded and
yet feels secure. A quick–tempered person does foolish things,
and the one who devises evil schemes is hated.*

PROVERBS 14:16–17

Do to others as you would have them do to you.

LUKE 6:31

*So in everything, do to others what you would have them
do to you, for this sums up the Law and the Prophets.*

MATTHEW 7:12

If either of you have a problem in controlling anger, find out the root cause of the anger and come up with solutions. Seek counsel if it seems appropriate. Pray for, and with each other, to keep anger out of your relationship and home. Your home should be a sanctuary you look forward to coming to.

Discuss with each other how you would like your spouse to treat you. You may be surprised at some of your spouse's answers. Listen sincerely and find ways to give your spouse what he or she desires.

Get rid of all bitterness, rage and anger, brawling
and slander, along with every form of malice.
Be kind and compassionate to one another,
forgiving each other, just as in Christ God forgave you.
EPHESIANS 4:31–32

Day 26

Being Critical

You, then, why do you judge your brother or sister?
Or why do you treat them with contempt?
For we will all stand before God's judgment seat.

ROMANS 14:10

Why do you look at the speck of sawdust in your brother's
eye and pay no attention to the plank in your own eye?
How can you say to your brother,
'Brother, let me take the speck out of your eye,'
when you yourself fail to see the plank in your own eye?
You hypocrite, first take the plank out of your eye, and then you
will see clearly to remove the speck from your brother's eye.

LUKE 6:41–42

Do not judge, or you too will be judged.

MATTHEW 7:1

The Bible has much to say about us judging each other. We all are on a different level in growth either in God, or not. Jesus wants us to focus on our own agenda with Him, and let Him worry about others. In John 20:22–23 Peter, concerned, asked Jesus, "What about him?" Jesus told him, "If I want him to remain alive until I return, what is that to you? You must follow me." Our chief concern should be how we stand up or fall in our walk with God.

A mark of our growth in our relationship with God is that we are closer to Him now than when we first started.

For many of us, it is very easy to point out issues with other people, no matter how large or small. We may not know their whole story, or care to look. We just like having the satisfaction of 'helping' them by letting them know how inferior they are to us. Love considers another's feelings. Jesus instructs us to find our own faults and work on them instead of 'fixing' others first. When we decide to take on God's job of being judgmental, especially not knowing all the facts, and think we are above the other, what results in are building walls instead of bridges—not only with those we have criticized—but with God himself. God is for those who humble themselves, and sets himself against the proud.

> *Therefore let us stop passing judgment on one another.*
> *Instead, make up your mind not to put any stumbling*
> *block or obstacle in the way of a brother or sister.*
> ROMANS 14:13

Don't be quick to criticize your spouse. Examine yourself and see if you have any areas in which you should improve. If your spouse needs help such as to overcome a bad habit such as smoking or swearing, then don't smoke or swear around your spouse. Support and build up your spouse and encourage him or her. Let your thoughts be of love. Instead of seeing the negative in your spouse, look at the positive things. Make a list of what you like about your spouse (the longer the list, the better) and give it to each other. Hang them up where you both can see it and can add to it through the years.

For in the same way you judge others, you will be judged,
and with the measure you use, it will be measured to you.

MATTHEW 7:2

What goes around comes around. We want people to see the best in us, but it starts first when we see the best in them.

Whatever is true, whatever is noble, whatever is right, whatever is pure, whatever is lovely, whatever is admirable —if anything is excellent or praiseworthy— think about such things.

PHILIPPIANS 4:8

Day 27

Destructive Attitudes

*Better a small serving of vegetables with love
than a fattened calf with hatred.*

PROVERBS 15:17

Relationships are crucial to our well-being—spiritually, emotionally and physically. To cultivate a good marriage is important to God because he loves us and knows if we take care of each other, we really are taking care of ourselves. He abhors it when one shows unkindness to another, and knows a couple who strive to make each other happy will weather the ups and downs of life together. Even though they may be poor, they will be happier together than a wealthy couple who cannot stand each other dining at the same table, regardless of how fine the meal is.

*Better a dry crust with peace and quiet than
a house full of feasting, with strife.*

PROVERBS 17:1

*But now you must rid yourselves of all such things as these: anger,
rage, malice, slander, and filthy language from your lips.*

59

*Do not lie to each other, since you have taken off your old
self with its practices and have put on the new self,
which is being renewed in knowledge in the image of its Creator.*

COLOSSIANS 3:8–10

Pride goes before destruction, a haughty spirit before a fall.

PROVERBS 16:18

Let us not become conceited, provoking and envying each other.

GALATIANS 5:26

*The house of the wicked will be destroyed, but
the tent of the upright will flourish.*

PROVERBS 14:11

*The house of the righteous contains great treasure, but
the income of the wicked brings them trouble.*

PROVERBS 15:6

The outside world can be mean, ugly, and harsh. If the world tears
you down, your spouse is there to build you up. Your home should
be a place you look forward to coming to, a loving sanctuary you
provide for each other.

This is true not just for physical aspects of a home, but also how
it is run by those who live in it. Taking the time to understand
your spouse and children, with their unique personalities, teaching
and applying biblical principles, and working <u>with</u> them to achieve
what is good for them and the home, you will build strong, loving
relationships that will strengthen over time. Any aspect of neglect
will weaken the foundation.

Day 28

The Price of Adultery

Marriage should be honored by all, and the marriage bed kept pure,
for God will judge the adulterer and all the sexually immoral.

HEBREWS 13:4

Brother and sisters, if someone is caught in a sin, you who
live by the Spirit should restore that person gently.
But watch yourselves, or you also may be tempted.

GALATIANS 6:1

In Proverbs, the father urges his son to protect himself by avoiding the temptation of committing adultery and to save himself from the destruction that follows. He knows that the real intimacy and pleasure that God intended in marriage and for families is destroyed in the adulterous relationship, and that those who commit the sin will be led to many kinds of deaths emotionally and spiritually, and miss out on the real joy of married love.

Many are tempted by giving into a fantasy. A fantasy can be fleeting. A few moments of giving into ideal pleasure can result into a lifetime of pain—a family is destroyed, a disease is caught. Satan promised one thing but delivered another. The satisfaction promised turned into embarrassment, and an irreparable fall. We often see it happen to politicians, but it also happens on the home front. When a family life is destroyed, the repercussions can fall into the work arena and affect the job performance. One can lose their family and job.

In Proverbs 5 and 6 the father tells his son,

> *"For a prostitute can be had for a loaf of bread, but*
> *another man's wife preys on your very life.*
> *Can a man scoop fire into his lap*
> *without his clothes being burned?*
> *Can a man walk on hot coals*
> *without his feet being scorched?*
> *So is he who sleeps with another man's wife;*
> *no one who touches her will go unpunished."*
>
> PROVERBS 6:26–29

He further tells him,

> *"But a man who commits adultery has no sense;*
> *whoever does so destroys himself.*
> *Blows and disgrace are his lot,*
> *and his shame will never be wiped away."*
>
> PROVERBS 6:32–33

He encourages instead,

> *"May your fountain be blessed,*
> *and may you rejoice in the wife of your youth.*
> *A loving doe, a graceful deer—*
> *may her breasts satisfy you always,*
> *may you ever be intoxicated with her love.*
> *Why, my son, be intoxicated with another man's wife?*
> *Why embrace the bosom of a wayward woman?"*

PROVERBS 5:18–20

The Bible speaks of not only physical death, but of spiritual death. Spiritual death is the separation from God and leads to the decay of our innermost being.

Trespassing and sin both mean going where we shouldn't go and can lead to many kinds of deaths. How can it make us dead? When we sin, we separate ourselves from God. Without God we start to decay. We can become deeply depressed. When we do something wrong, we constantly look over our shoulder in fear of getting caught. We start to spin webs of lies. We lose peace, and toss and turn at night. If we commit adultery, we break up a family, and risk getting a disease that can kill us, as well as our spouse. We can do so many wrong things we become numb to what is right.

Day 29

Marriage is Intended to be Permanent

By law a married woman is bound to her husband
as long as he is alive, but if her husband dies, she is
released from the law that binds her to him.

ROMANS 7:2

Some Pharisees came to test Jesus about marriage.
They asked, "Is it lawful for a man to divorce
his wife for any and every reason?"
"Haven't you read," he replied, "that at the beginning
the Creator 'made them male and female,' and said,
'For this reason a man will leave his father and mother
and be united to his wife, and the two will become one flesh'?
So they are no longer two, but one flesh.
Therefore what God has joined together, let no one separate."

MATTHEW 19:3–6

The verse "Therefore what God has joined together, let no one separate" is commonly used in the closure of a wedding ceremony.

God designed marriage to be a permanent, deep and meaningful union between a couple to share the joys and hardships of life together, and for their children to experience a solid home with a firm foundation. The world outside God's realm makes it easy for a couple to be separated. In some states a divorce can be granted without a waiting period, and based on "irreconcilable differences." No real reason is needed.

The world influences many through the media, movies, television and their own reasoning that it is okay to be separated. People often hear of a husband leaving his wife for a younger woman, and a bored woman leaving her husband for a more exciting life. Hearts have turned to stone. Those who willingly turn their backs on God go into a cold and uncaring world with no guarantees.

His protective and loving laws are designed to provide a rich, fulfilling life and relationship. At times it takes hard work, but less work than dealing with the consequences of pain from chasing empty dreams and producing broken lives.

Day 30

Divorce

So be on your guard, and do not be unfaithful
to the wife of your youth.
The man who hates and divorces his wife,"
says the Lord, the God of Israel,
"does violence to the one he should protect," says the
Lord Almighty.
So be on your guard, and do not be unfaithful.

MALACHI 2:16

⌒

Let love and faithfulness never leave you; bind them around
your neck, write them on the tablet of your heart.

PROVERBS 3:3

God abhors mistreatment, violence, and destructive attitudes in a relationship which lead to divorce. Divorce is a result of hate. It causes dissension, separation, defiles what He has created for good, breaks up the foundation of the home, deteriorates the health mentally, physically and spiritually, and unfaithfulness breaks the bond of trust.

If you look up the word violence in a dictionary you'll find it described as behavior involving physical force intended to hurt, damage, or kill someone or something, and as the strength of emotion or an unpleasant or destructive natural force, or as a swift and intense force.

God, as the author of love and life, knows the ugly acts that are involved in divorce which mar the intent He designed for a couple. Divorce represents decay and death. Some never can recover from it, nor their children. Children of divorced parents can be traumatized by it, and the secure foundation they thought they had has been shattered.

Fifty years ago it used to be children with divorced parents often felt uncomfortable in a classroom because divorce was uncommon, and would notice other children whisper around them. It is the opposite today. Many children have parents that are divorced and it is considered common.

The Millennial generation are marrying later. Some of it is due to women wanting to wait until after they get their degree, but for others it is fear. Because of their divorced parents, or seeing so many of their friends' parents divorce, the concept of marriage has lost its appeal and value.

Amy Desai, J.D., in her article "How Could Divorce Affect My Kids?" published in focusonthefamily.com, listed how children are affected from research comparing the children of divorced parents to children with married parents. She revealed that children from divorced homes suffer academically. They experience high levels of behavioral problems, they are more likely to be incarcerated for committing a crime as a juvenile. Because the custodial parent's income typically drops substantially, the children are almost five times more likely to live in poverty, and teens are much more likely to engage in drug and alcohol use, as well as have sexual intercourse.

Proverbs 11:29 reveals what happens to those who bring troubles upon their family and ruin the home – they inherit the wind. They gain nothing, and there isn't anything left to hold on to.

HOPE FOR THE
BROKEN HOME

Day 31

If my people, who are called by my name, will
humble themselves and pray and seek my face
and turn from their wicked ways,
then will I hear from heaven
and will forgive their sin
and will heal their land.

2 CHRONICLES 7:14

When we sincerely regret what we have done wrong and mourn over the pain we have caused, God wants us to make amends and reconcile. Especially in families. Broken homes and broken relationships lead to broken hearts and lives. What breaks our hearts breaks God's. He is a merciful God, and the God who gives second, even third chances. He wants to give us every opportunity to right a wrong because He knows when bridges are built instead of walls, love grows. In order to grow closer to God, and experience His power in your life, make it a priority to reconcile yourself with those you need to, to fully be reconciled with God.

Pride can prevent us from wanting to find ways to build bridges of love to restore the relationship, but joy comes to those who are willing to please God and make amends. Each new day is an opportunity to serve each other, and God, better. All involved will experience healing and reap the rewards of kindness, mercy and cherished love.

Because of God, our life is not hopeless. When we turn to Him, He restores us. He instantly forgives. He doesn't drum his fingers and say, "Oh, let me think about this. I recall you also did this, this, and this." He says He forgives and remembers our sins no more. "I, even I, am He who blots out your transgressions for My own sake; And I will not remember your sins" (Isaiah 43:25).

People wanted to stone an adultress to death. Christ called them on it and said the person who never sinned should cast the first stone. No one did. After they all left he told her to go and sin no more.

By wisdom a house is built, and through
understanding it is established;
through knowledge its rooms are filled with
rare and beautiful treasures.
PROVERBS 24:3–4

1. What kind of treasures are in a home? For example– love, harmony, peace, and more. List as many as you can think of, and share your list with your spouse. Discuss ways to make your list a reality.
2. How can having knowledge enrich a home?

It is never too late to repent, never a wrong time to make the right move, never a bad time to do good and to turn things around.

LOVE IN THE HOME

Love is patient
We all have our shortcomings.

Love is kind
We are kind to each other.

It does not envy
Do not give jealousy room,
And be thankful for what we have.

It does not boast
We don't place ourselves above another,
nor do we put others down.

It is not proud.
We can celebrate and be proud of each other's
accomplishments, but being arrogant is wrong.

It is not rude
Derogatory comments, put-downs, sarcastic and
hurtful language is not allowed in our home.

It is not self-seeking
We look out for each other.

It is not easily angered
We control our attitude, thoughts and words.

It keeps no record of wrongs
Forgive, forget, restore and move on.

Love does not delight in evil
Evil is defined as harmful, hateful or destructive action.

But rejoices with the truth
Deceit and lies conceal and lead to destruction,
the truth reveals, upholds and prevails.

It always protects
We have each other's back.

Always trusts
We trust each other with our belongings, our feelings
and concerns, our plans, our lives.

Always hopes
Life isn't perfect, nor are any of us,
but we strive for a betterment.

Always perseveres
Don't give up.

Love never fails
Hate tears apart and destroys, love builds up,
conquers and unites.

---

1 Corinthians 13:4–8 are words in bold.

If problems come up, we work together with love to seek solutions. The goal is to make our home a sanctuary, a place we can feel comfortable in and with each other. If the world gives us a bad day, we have a place where we can feel safe, and experience real love, joy, comfort and peace.

Above all, love each other deeply.

1 PETER 4:8

Notes

Notes

Notes

Notes

Notes

Printed in the United States
By Bookmasters